RETIREME

The shortest guide ever

An easy read, it covers the issues around retirement and lets you move forward with confidence

Michael Carter

CONTENTS

Hangin' around   3

WARNING   5

Preparation   7
     a. Continue working   9
     b. Slowing down / Consulting   11
     c. Expand a hobby   13
     d. Set up a business   16
     e. Do some community good   18
     f. Travel, travel, travel   20
     g. Move abroad   23
     h. Rest and with whom   25

Financial planning
     a. Income & outgoings   27
     b. Pensions and capital   29
     c. Family and Inheritance Tax   32
     d. Equity release/downsizing   34
     e. Sheltered accommodation and healthcare   37

Plan B
     a. Last will and testament   40
     b. A living will   43
     c. Provision for other(s)   45
     d. Falling over – wake-up call   47
     e. Level living   50
     f. No time to die   52

Happy retirement   55

HANGIN' AROUND

Do you ever stop and wonder what your purpose in life is?

Sure you might have procreated, and thus saved humanity from extinction - but that was the first half of your life. So what's the second half for?

There is no obvious role. If everyone shuffled off their mortal coils immediately after their son/daughter/no assigned gender's graduation would the world be better? It would certainly pass wealth on far sooner and probably more of it too as doubtless in the second half 'Ski' (spending kids' inheritance) outweighs capital accumulation, or does it? That might need closer examination, later.

Early determination would also lead to a lesser burden on health resources and social care. It would eliminate the need for state pensions and other age related welfare.

It's beginning to look like a good idea - but are there any downsides? There seem to be two. Firstly, the emotional appeal: 'I have worked hard for forty something years, now I believe I have earned my retirement.' Secondly, the world revolves around conspicuous consumption so how would Apple, for instance, cope with only 50% of the demand for its iPhones?

In earth's recent history - since the invention of money - it has largely been the premise you would work on, past the halfway line of life but through seniority and/or shedding financial responsibility for the next generation, producing a situation where income exceeded need, you therefore enjoyed later life. More recently still we introduced a pension line where, you could cross it at a certain age, then actually stop work and be paid by pension to continue life.

The 'pension line' as measured, hasn't changed much since its introduction, but the piece beyond, for the average human has increased from 'n' weeks to 'n' years. Thanks to better health, environment and habits the piece beyond is now of material significance and now needs careful consideration where once was but a bonus.

So what then are the golden rules for enjoying those final years?

- Preparation
- Financial planning
- Planning for it
- Planning it out
- Plan B

But before we go a step further:

WARNING   WARNING WARNING

A lot of this will involve money that hopefully you have either accumulated yourself or have built up in a pension pot. Probably aside from the house you live in, it represents most of your wealth or at least the expected source of your future retirement income.

You are a natural to be targeted by all-manner of rogues and scoundrels, whose sole purpose is to make what is yours, theirs. So DO NOT EVER encourage unsolicited conversations about your retirement planning, accept that good advice is NOT FREE and if it seems too good to be true, IT PROBABLY IS.

Secondly, however sound suggestions appear to be in this book, the author could err or the legislation on which it is based, changed. So before making any commitment to anything, please seek INDEPENDENT FINANCIAL ADVICE.

Finally, even after making a well-advised decision, always give yourself some breathing space to reflect, before the final irreversible commitment.

That said, the author intends that the rest of this book gives you useful insights and in turn leads to better decisions for the future. There is only one serious roadblock to a proper future life plan...

...How long will you live.

PREPARATION

The military has it right. Its seven Ps: "Proper Prior Planning Prevents Piss Poor Performance" absolutely apply to retirement preparation as much as battle planning. However as we have already seen, there is one variable that makes the certainty of proper prior preparation a complete nonsense, that is how long you are going to live.

You might be part of that rare element of society with a terminal illness, know you have it and some quality third party provided, accurate knowledge of your life expectancy. Otherwise as with the rest of us mere mortals, our only clues are the fact that death is one of the oft quoted two certainties in life (the other being 'taxes') and the fact that is statistically unlikely we will die on the date predicted by annuity tables.

So preparation is about preparing for both the expected and the unexpected.

Many people regard their official retirement age as a finishing line. Break through the tape and hey-ho one is retired. This focussed mind-set comes with an enormous number of potential *elephants in the room*, ranging from 'Can you afford to stop?', 'Can the business you are in let you go just like that?' through to 'What next?'

The answers to these, and other conundrums should come out in the next few chapters, so please patiently read on, ideally to the end of the book before committing firmly to any particular course of action. That's because a lot of your many options interlock – usually to your advantage.

And please also regard this book as a huge signpost. If any direction of travel from it looks promising, do dive into a search engine on the Internet and look deeper into whichever subject it is. But again as per the warning on the earlier pages, do not commit to a course of action with a website unless you are completely happy with its bona fides. Do seek an independent financial advisor, ideally from your community, ideally by personal recommendation, not a result of a web search. It is not wrong to ask others if they have a recommendation and if you come up short, you could ask your bank or your local Citizens Advice Bureau. There are over 300 such bureaux in the UK with volunteers offering free impartial advice.

PREPARATION (a) Continue working

So let's first consider that you simply work through your official retirement age and carry on. Since 2006 it has been unlawful to discriminate on age, so your employer normally has no grounds to cease to employ you, just because you've reached a certain age.

> If you feel you are being discriminated for age (or for sex, race etc) in your employment, then react promptly. The law of the land requires you initiate action through any grievance procedure with your employer and if unsatisfactory, with an Employment Tribunal. In the latter case *promptly* means the Tribunal must be made aware within three months of the first discrimination.

Continuing to work on could be because:

- You enjoy the work
- Like many people you need structure – which work can provide
- Your employer has requested it – maybe you have unique skills and knowledge
- You need the money
- You've not made another decision.

There are some immediate advantages in carrying on. For a start you'll stop paying National Insurance contributions, so your take home pay will increase. If you don't immediately take your state pension, it will increase in value for when you do – over and above any normal inflation increases. Finally in terms of money, you will probably be a net saver, as opposed to spender if you continue to take salary.

Those are monetary advantages. As noted above you may carry on because you enjoy your work. And it may be more than the work itself. Are your work colleagues also some of your better friends? Do you enjoy talking not only with them but with suppliers and customers of your business? Maybe you just like to be out of your house for the forty or so waking hours you commute and work each week? Maybe you are something like an architect – work for you is a creative opportunity?

It is often the case that your employer hasn't comprehended properly and with enough forethought about the gap your departure could cause. So whether you are retiring on the first possible day or at an agreed date beyond that, plans should be developed and then implemented to transition your skill set to another person or to reorganise the work so that your position ceases to be critical to the business. Whilst you might regard this as your employer's responsibility – which it is – it is really sensible if you don't want to be retained post a date you've set, to chivvy your employer to ensure steps necessary are actually taken in good time.

PREPARATION (b) Slowing down / Consulting

Cutting your days of work down initially to four and then sometime later to three etc is a textbook way of easing yourself into retirement. But two matters immediately spring to mind. Firstly what are you going to use the extra day(s) outside of work for. We are not dealing with this immediately, but will before you finish the book. Secondly, your employer will almost certainly pro-rata your salary whilst undoubtedly it will be your smarts that are continued to be employed 100%. In fact the piece of work *lost* when you cut your hours is likely to be that work that is of least economic value as well as some of your watercooler moments.

Think about it. When you phone for a plumber for a domestic emergency, his or her call out charge and hourly rate are towards exorbitant. So naturally you will do the clearing up after him / her so as not to make the total charge mind-blowing. The plumber is charging you for a short piece of skilled work – founded on years of prior experience and training – rather than a pro-rata allocation of an hour (or whatever) of his working week.

The author would argue the case that like you employing the plumber , your employer is using you. So as an alternative to putting your employed working week successively through the slicer – losing a day a week here, a day a week there…) you leave completely and then offer your services back to your employer based on an hourly or daily consulting fee instead? This, subject to the tax-man, would make you an independent consultant being paid as and when required by your ex-employer *provided it suited you too.* At risk is the fact they wouldn't use you as much as you expected or perhaps needed, but on the plus side you'd be free to offer similar services to other businesses too.

HMRC aka the tax-man does not like employees leaving employment and then becoming independent consultants for the same employer. HMRC has created and strengthened a test known as IR35 to determine if you are legitimately independent or an employee in a different guise. More over time, the rules are tightening, so if following this route, look up IR35 and if necessary ask your ex-employee to process your invoices for your time working for them through its payroll and be self-employed for others.

If you are going this route you will need a hourly or daily charging rate. This new you will need to pay yourself for holidays, sick and time spent winning additional business and the more mundane administration of raising invoices, chasing for payment etc. Absent any more meaningful data ,how about assuming 250 working days a year and divide your previous annual salary by that *and then double it.* Initially your ex employer might baulk at that price but you need to tell them about all the other pieces to this and remind them that they'll only be paying for the more valuable parts of what you do and not to sweep the floor nor attend their Xmas parties and so on.

PREPARATION (c) Expand a hobby

We've touched on easing up or stopping work so we should now begin to look at the other half of the work-life balance. What are you going to do with the extra time you find yourself with if you retire, or even simply reduce your hours or days of work?

The most obvious thought is surely to do more of something you already regard as a hobby or interest. Slightly less obvious, but more beneficial might be to do something that keeps your brain active and / or your body fit. The Internet is full of ideas but most sources coalesce around a list of options like this:

- Creative
- Gardening
- Yoga and fitness
- Birding
- Reading
- TV and Cinema

And the list goes on. Sleeping often appears in the top 20 or so of many lists and obviously the lists can be quite long depending upon the granularity of the ideas. 'Creative' can easily be divided into art, craft, knitting, needlework, woodwork, model-making... A lot of people would say 'walking' should be high on any list, but if it is any indication, the Royal Society for the Protection of Birds (RSPB) has over ten times the membership of the Ramblers Association.

Let's consider the expansion of something you already do. Suppose you already play Bridge once a week. In retirement do you want to play every day or is once a week going to be the continuing right level for you? Do you enjoy gardening enough to think about acquiring an allotment to add to your capacity for growing things quite apart from all the extra energy you will expend and the arising health benefits? Are you a keen railway modeller and is now the time to create a new portable layout with the view to both display and the opportunity to win prizes in competitions organised by your local club?

Think what you do now as a hobby and do a little blue-sky thinking about where that could lead to. Then ask yourself if you want to attempt that journey or that at the present level, it provides enough of whatever for your enjoyment.

If you are not expanding an existing hobby, you will have capacity to take on another one. Please try others, but *please try before you buy*. Suppose it's beer-making or pottery. For the former equipment to make five gallons (approx. 25 litres) of beer is not expensive and likewise attending a pottery class or workshop is not going to be costly. But proper brewing equipment for the former and a kiln and wheel for the latter are expensive investments which should only be made once *you know* it is a true interest. Even then, you might consider the economics of purchasing second-hand rather than new?

Others to try include those you might not expect to be doing because of pre-conceived prejudices. There is no reason at all why men don't do crocheting and knitting – two very popular leisure activities, nor why women don't join walking football teams or make model aeroplanes etc.

PREPARATION (d) Set up a business

The UK is quite a strange place from a legal point of view. Very little written law exists as to setting up in business. Obviously without appropriate qualifications you can't establish yourself as a professional such as a doctor, lawyer or accountant, but beyond that the only requirement to apply for a licence to trade appears to be to run a pub or open a sex shop! Therefore if you want to start a business – you can just start, which is not the case in most other countries.

The other conundrum is 'when do you start?' If you collect stamps and sell duplicates to acquire others, are you a stamp dealer and should you account for the profits as a trade? Probably not. 'Starting' is not defined in law, though there is much common law ie legal cases, which provide pointers. Probably, to keep it simple, you should regard it yourself as starting when you deliberately seek to make a profit from an enterprise rather than as a incidental activity to a hobby or clearing your personal junk in a car-boot sale or similar.

As a word to the wise, if you are thinking of an enterprise, start keeping receipts of any expenditure you incur from the moment the thinking begins. It is perfectly acceptable for costs to exceed revenues and a business loss can be set against other income and reduce your income tax bill. It is also important to log your business travel. HMRC allows you to claim 45p per business mile as a legitimate cost if driving a car and even 20p per mile by bicycle

Also, as with a hobby it is important you *try before you buy*. Suppose you want to run some sort of retail operation. Before you commit unrecoverable sums to your own venture, try the business out with or for someone else already doing it. Most independent traders need a break once in a while, so approach one in your proposed business area and offer to be holiday relief to run the business whilst they laze in the sun or whatever. Chances are you will be able to negotiate at least minimum wage for it *and* get conclusive hands-on experience to prove to yourself whether you are going to like it for real. Whatever your business you will almost invariably have to do some selling. If that's not been your forte to date, the all-important car boot sale raises its head again – it is a great test bed to see if you can sell. This time not clearing your junk but maybe pot plants or homemade chocolate brownies or something – it doesn't have to be what you intend as your business, its simply the chance to prove you can sell.

"Aha…" I hear you shout, "…mine's a web business so no sales are required." Who are you fooling? Ask yourself firstly how are people going to find your site on the web and then secondly once there, why are they going to buy from you? Does your product really sell itself or do you have to promote and even answer questions about it?

PREPARATION (e) Do some community good

A headteacher known to the author, recently retired and wanted to do something voluntary. When asked what, she replied "Anything that doesn't involve bl**dy kids". Fortunately, the not-for-profit sector when involving volunteers, rarely seeks prior experience in the area concerned. You don't need a degree to rattle a collecting tin, you don't need retail experience to work in a charity shop, or warehouse experience to pack parcels in a food bank. It might help if you have a little financial knowledge to be a treasurer of one of the approximately 166,000 charities in the UK but even then most treasurers seem to have to account for less than £5,000 per year and copying the previous Treasurer's efforts is often enough.

You probably won't have to rattle a collecting tin. Most charities are much more sophisticated and rely on online contributions and legacies. The individuals who accost you on the street and want you to pledge £3-5 or more per month – the so called 'charity muggers' are rarely volunteers. It is paid work, available to you if you want it, but can you be that endlessly excited to talk to total strangers all day with the same limited word sales pitch?

In total UK charities collect almost £50bn a year in income. Overwhelmingly from people prepared to give money to the cause *so someone else can do that charity's work.* This means there are almost always openings for volunteers in every charity. So without making it mercenary, pick a charity you would like to help and offer your services. Even if its website says 'volunteers are not currently wanted' the chances are the website is not up to date, and anyway your skills might be just what they want.

But be careful. Someone known to the author volunteered as a school governor and attended monthly meetings. Fifteen years later, as chair of the governors, it required daily attendance at the school. Likewise despite offering to stand down as treasurer of a walking group at each AGM, the author was re-elected unopposed 20 years in a row.

Another consideration is size and bureaucracy. The top 1,000 charities – the ones you have most likely heard of - are really giant corporations. Oxfam for instance (at time of writing) has around 650 shops which run with about 26,000 volunteers. On that scale there will have to be a lot of rules and governance considerations and a volunteer will be expected to be bound by them. Sure volunteering for a larger charity helps the charity, but the volunteer can't really expect to contribute anything beyond being a small cog in a large machine. If however you have the zeal and zest to want to go and change things you should aim for a much smaller, local charity. Even then, and here's the author talking from bitter experience, many charity committees are composed of individuals who find preserving the status quo in their affairs often more important than the ideals of the charity. Perhaps another case of *try before you buy?*

PREPARATION (f) Travel, travel, travel

It's all a matter of budget. There is a ship – MS The World - basically built as a 165 apartment village on the ocean but with the other things you'd expect from a cruise ship in terms of restaurants, bars, spa and pool etc, as well. It slowly travels the world, its destinations determined by the residents who typically live a tax-free life. Residents are not normally named but apparently they include Arnold Schwarzenegger and Madonna. On that basis you probably can't afford to sell up on land and move aboard for the rest of your life?

UK cruise ships often have cabins below £100 per night on their itineraries so multiplied out that is £36,500 per year before you negotiate handsome discounts if you were to base yourself aboard. That's a fraction of the price of The World, but still offers full board and lodging and mostly all drinks are included. Still expensive? Yes but think of all the costs you would avoid by not maintaining a home – and you could sell your house and have that as cash to help with the bill.

Of course other forms of travel are available. Air is the most common where after n hours in a cramped tube you emerge at a destination. And that is destination singular – whereas cruise ships offer a variety of destinations. 'Not exactly true...' you say, '...from the destination airport you can surely travel on extensively?' One can, but do you? A great place to go would be Costa Rica for example – a pleasant climate, they speak English extensively, crime is low and the hotels clean and efficient. But when you go and 'do' Costa Rica how far does one venture? To the four corners or simply a multi-centre break? Stay in the country or venture into next door Nicaragua or Panama?

If you are going to choose travel as your retirement gift to yourself, then try to think beyond 'packages' and simply *out and back*. If you go the 5,420 miles to Costa Rica – make it a one or two month excursion rather than a number of short stays with repeated inter-continental air travel.

Beyond sea and air, we have railways, cars and for those with the passion: motor-bikes and bicycles. For most of these, it is about a journey. Maybe the trans-Siberian railway or (motor)cycling across the USA? If a journey like those was done in your younger days you would be time constrained – by needing to be back at work. Done in retirement the speed element is no longer present so you have time to enjoy the places you travel through as much as the journey itself. The trans-Siberian for instance takes seven days straight through for its 6,152 miles. Why not jump off at various points for a couple of days at a time and learn a little about Russia and its people instead of noting seven days of just lakes, trees and scrub?

Notwithstanding all the nonsense of 'be at the airport at least two hours before departure' etc, travel is still great fun. However as you probably know, the UK health service doesn't extend beyond the Isles of Scilly so travel insurance is vital. You will also appreciate premiums rise rapidly as people grow older – so if you are faced with a large premium and can talk to a human, ask about the availability of discount for higher excesses. If you can afford to bear the first £250 or £500 of a claim, it takes you out of the area which consumes most insurers' time and thus should provide a cheaper premium for you.

PREPARATION (g) Move abroad

If ever there was a real case of *try before you buy*, it is when you plan to up sticks and move country. Long before a huge and probably irreversible decision, you should go to your proposed destination and rent – ideally for several months. Even before that some desktop research should be applied to make sure you know (and like – or at least appreciate) how you will be treated health-wise at your proposed destination, how taxes work on income, property and assets, how property is acquired, how you will find the different climate and perhaps how you will cope with a different language. Don't overlook there are often different rules applying to residents rather than simply visitors. You might need to apply for residency, register to vote and pay taxes, do a local driving test to be awarded a local licence etc.

It might help if you make a list of the things that come to mind and find out how each one is dealt with at your proposed destination. Whatever you do, don't simply assume British rules apply. Some countries impose unusual taxes on things that don't in the UK. Some countries have different rules for the receipt of money from abroad. Likewise your UK drafted will might be invalid in the country you are going to and your carefully thought out plan for your demise overruled by local legislation.

When you do go on your trial rental mission, being there for any length of time will probably answer in practical terms, language and climate thoughts but will especially allow you to see a broad portfolio of properties for sale way beyond those that find their way into your search engine back at the home computer. More choice should mean a better deal and/or a much more *you* property.

And why are you picking a particular place anyway? It is often because of friends or family in the area. If it is, are they routed there or might they in fact move out for whatever reason even as you move in? Then you'll be faced with making new friends and connections – which is a little harder than knowing someone already but may turn out to be much better. Friends often materialise through social activities, so if for instance you are keen golfer will your destination's golf club welcome you to membership? You enjoy playing Bridge – is there a club or group you'll be able to join or otherwise create a foursome?

PREPARATION (h) Rest and with whom

What is your marital status? Statistically at this point you are one of a couple but you could be single (including widowed or divorced). If you are going to *retire and rest* as this chapter presupposes – the first question is with whom? Alone? You might want to pair up with a sibling or friend. Whilst it not quite true 'two can live as cheaply as one', there are a lot of savings if you only need one dwelling between two, perhaps one car, one set of bills and one set of meals to make etc. If you're a sociable single man, given the greater life expectancy of women, you could be very popular if your resting is in an area congregated by older folk. As a single woman, you probably find it easier than a man to make new friends as (again statistically) women tend to be more sociable.

Complications occur if you are a couple – married, same sex, just friends or whatever if the desire to retire and rest is more strongly held by one than the other. This can be particularly prevalent where there is a large age gap between the two of you and where one still wants to dance the light fantastic, whilst the other wants to hang up his / her shoes.

This can be a big elephant in the room. Suppose the elder one of a pair wants to retire to say Spain. You both have enjoyed Spain on holidays and you are both able to communicate quite well in Spanish so it seems a natural development to the elder. But it might mean the younger one being expected to give up employment he / she enjoys before retirement age and with little prospect of picking up a similar role, post relocation. That can be a wrench in the best of times. So it is important to communicate with each other almost as soon as the idea occurs and make sure the other half is in broad agreement with exploring the idea into a plan and in doing the plan to journey together.

Even without an age difference, retire and rest will almost certainly mean spending a lot more time together in each other's presence. So if you are a recent coming together, you might very well want to again *try before you buy* in so far as spending some concentrated time together before uprooting either of you from what he / she had before. Perhaps a cruise of a few weeks duration?

There is also the slightly tangential aspect of moving in with someone, even a couple of miles away from where you've lived a chunk of your life, might involuntarily or unexpectedly change a number of your previous 'rocks' be it friends, neighbours, local pub, access to your allotment etc. Things you had otherwise anticipated as continuing *as normal* into your retirement.

FINANCIAL PLANNING (a) Income & outgoings

(Sir) Max Hastings was despatched as a war reporter to the Falklands Argie-Bargy in 1982 with several thousand troops on the QE2. During the long days at sea he would interview ordinary squaddies and asked one what he regarded as the most dangerous thing ahead of him. Instantly the soldier replied: "An officer with a map."

If your circumstances are going to change at your proposed retirement date – and by that *circumstances* really means income – then you need to map out with confidence an annual budget for your future. This has to cover both income and outgoings.

Income will include any ongoing salary, any private pension, your state pension and other income eg from savings, investments, business ventures and part-time work. Please don't forget that passing pension age will stop you paying National Insurance but most sources of income – including state pension – are subject to income tax.

Outgoings should include the cost of your home ie mortgage if continuing, council tax and bills (insurance, utilities, telephone, internet…) plus reasonable sums for normal travel (car, bus, train…) and then some for food, drink, meals out, clothing and pets. Remember if you are not travelling to work each day post retirement, your travel costs should be much lower and in any event at normal retirement age you should be entitled to a concessionary travel pass from your local council (in London from age 60).

There hopefully is a positive difference between you total income and total outgoings. This sum contributes to holidays and discretionary expenditure like helping out the next generation. If it is negative and you vetted it for obvious mistakes, then you know your savings will have to support you going forward.

Many people plan that their mortgages are paid off by their retirement date – so if this includes you, you can exclude it from your sums. If however you have a repayment mortgage that continues some way past your retirement date, you need to factor it in to your outgoings. But then cheer yourself by making your income and expenditure plan a multi-year one and include the first year with no mortgage to pay off. If however your mortgage is interest only, have you considered how you are going to pay off the balance at the end of the term? Historically mortgage lenders have been happy to renew this arrangement almost regardless of circumstances and are prohibited from making decisions solely on age. But the era of excess is now long gone and one's ability to continue with new *interest only* mortgages as an existing one expires is now subject to increased scrutiny – particularly around ability to pay both interest and the capital sum at the end of the term. But don't panic, please – have a read of the chapter on downsizing and equity release.

FINANCIAL PLANNING (b) Pensions and capital

In your rapid journey through life you have possibly collected a number of pensions particularly if you have worked for a number of employers. Now is probably the time to round them all up.

Historically many employees were in defined benefit 'final salary schemes' where you earned a pension based on your final year's salary, or if you left before retirement age, your service to that point. Where defined benefit schemes still exist, 'final' has almost completely been replaced by 'average salary schemes' – as the name implies, based on average salary over your working period. If you have had one of these at any point in your career, you should have annual updates from your employer, even if you left a while ago. If you don't have annual notification, re-establish contact with your old employer. If the business has folded, go online for details of the free Pensions Tracing Service as the liquidation of a business should not mean the end of its pension fund. But note, and try and remember. Before 1988 it was often the case on leaving to receive a refund of contributions and no built up pension entitlement. So maybe your final pay cheque was generous and saved your employer a future obligation to you.

For most employers today, defined benefit has moved to defined contribution , that is you will receive a pension based on what you and your employer's contributions to a fund will buy at retirement. You might have several of these 'pots' usually held by insurance companies, if you have had several employers. You could have your own SIPP (self-invested pension plan). For all these it is worth checking how much in total you can withdraw as a lump sum – should you need it and as well, what the sums will buy you in terms of a pension. If you do have more than one pot, you should think about combining them as larger sums of money can give you the benefit of scale and better negotiating power. A good Independent Financial Advisor set on this task will probably earn his fee and still obtain a better deal for you than you doing it yourself.

But what pension? When you buy one – as an annuity – you will need to decide whether it should be a level sum for ever, or starting lower and rising, if there should be a half pension for someone else should you die first and if you want a guaranteed minimum of five years' worth, whether you die or not. It's a formidable mix and whilst circumstances might determine some of the choices, ultimately it will be your choice and the resultant pension a function of those choices.

Last but possibly not least, is your state pension.

If you visit: https://www.gov.uk/check-state-pension you can find out what your forecasted state pension will be, when you can expect to start receiving it and what you can do if it less than the maximum, to top it up.

Whilst rules change, at the time of writing the top up scheme known as 'buying additional years' represented a very good value investment where circa £700 paid in gave you about £2 per week extra – about 14% pa on your money -though of course you don't ever get the £700 back.

Please remember all pensions are treated as income and are taxable. After normal retirement age (as set by the government) you no longer pay National Insurance but you do still benefit from a tax allowance that takes (in 2020/21) the first £12,500 annual earnings out of tax.

FINANCIAL PLANNING (c) Family and Inheritance Tax

You might think some of these chapters are out of sequence? How for instance can you schedule income and expenditure before you know what your pension is going to be? The problem is that a number of retirement topics are suddenly relevant to different people at different times – so best read all and then backtrack to what matters to you now.

So starting at the end of your life, your estate may be one of the 4% who collectively pay over £5bn a year to HMRC in Inheritance Tax - as a result of your death. As with most taxes, exemptions, exclusions and shifting rules mean that a whole book could be written on this tax alone. Indeed there are many and if it might affect you, please buy one. But first the idiots' guide. Passing your entire wealth to your other half is inheritance tax free. When they subsequently die – let's call that the taxable death - the first £650,000 - £1m is tax free (the extra £350,000 if there's a property involved). Shares in an unquoted business and holdings of agricultural land don't count, nor do donations to charities as well as gifts to anyone given more than seven years before the taxable death. There are many other rules but these few cover most circumstances.

If the taxable death occurs inside the seven years then the gift value is added to the estate – but there is a sliding scale applied on the normal tax rate of 40% applied above the exemption, which reduces the tax charge the longer ago the gift was given.

There are also *use them or lose them* annual exemptions of gifts given up to £3,000 per year and amounts for family members marrying etc. as well as gifts of any amount regularly given from income but where they don't reduce your standard of living. Far more details are on the web if you are a lucky one with cash to spare.

Let's concentrate on larger gifts. If you have surplus funds, over and above a lifestyle for you – then consider when a lump sum passed to the next generation is likely to be most use. The oft answer is 'now' is much better than 'later'. It is simple economics. The next generation have huge costs like house-buying and raising a family now, so some cash would really help, rather than a smaller sum later after the taxman has taken a slice. Then live for seven plus more years and there's no tax liability on them or your estate.

Be careful with your *gift*. Many retiring people want to gift their homes to the next generation, and that's fine. Whatever its value when you gift it, will go into a tax calculation if you don't last the seven years – otherwise no problem. Except the authorities don't regard it as a gift if you give it and then stay as a tenant in what was your house. Conditional gifts like this here are not regarded as you would hope.

But remember, giving to the next generation isn't a requirement or even an obligation. You could always SKI – Spend Kids Inheritance.

FINANCIAL PLANNING (d) Equity release/downsizing

Statistically you have probably brought up a family. You've probably moved three times in your life and the current house is the largest? And now your children have flown the nest and it's just the two of you? Why are you staying put? Could it be:

- It's nicely increasing in value
- It's conveniently located for, and large enough for, the family to visit
- All our friends are around and it's where our social life occurs
- It's near shops, hospital and/or transport
- We haven't thought about moving or it's too much hassle

Whilst the first four are plausible reasons, the last one smacks of inertia. Your house is probably your largest physical asset in money terms and represents a source of capital for potential use elsewhere.

One very popular option is to downsize. A smaller house probably better fits your needs – less to clean and maintain, smaller bills from Council Tax to electricity – and perhaps being a better citizen, releasing housing stock to those in need of larger space? And don't forget, having cost you less, you will end up with some extra cash. And apart from paying Stamp Duty on your new home, the taxman leaves the profit on what is termed your 'principal private residence' well alone.

Merge downsizing with opportunity and there are some possibly big upsides:

- Realise your dream to live in the country or by the coast
- Have the garden you've always wanted
- Move closer to your family

Any of these might be reason enough to take the plunge and move house.

But what if you want to stay? If we assume you own your home and your mortgage is paid off, then 100% of the equity is yours (and your partner's). You could release some cash perhaps by re-mortgaging your existing house but the problem then is you have to at the very least pay interest on the money and probably repayments of the capital as well. If you've got yourself some big pensions coming in, then demonstrably to a mortgage company you are a credible risk and not dependent on the vagaries of employment and if cash now beats cash when it arrives from the pension provider, this is a route forward.

Another route is equity release. As we have identified, you currently own 100% of the equity in the house and there are lenders out there – usually large insurance companies with pensions to pay out themselves – who will gladly invest in some of the equity in your home. They gain a valuation on your home, they reference life expectancy tables for the younger of the two owners (if you are a couple) and then offer you a sum of money that is not repayable in your lifetime. That sum and interest on the sum are rolled up, secured and only reclaimed, on the sale of the property following the second death. The interest rate is their ultimate profit. Any increase in the house's value will be for the benefit of your estate.

Because the lender for equity release has no certainty as to the time of your death, the implied interest rate is likely to be higher that the much publicised mortgages out there. But there are two rebuttals: firstly if you do think this is the way to go, shop around as rates vary enormously and secondly if the ultimate inheritance amount doesn't bother you, who cares? Note also, you will almost certainly have to use an independent financial advisor for equity release as few reputable companies will deal direct.

FINANCIAL PLANNING (e) Sheltered accommodation and healthcare

Which way do you want to go for later life accommodation? Private or State?

Whilst we have all hoped across our lifetime that state help in elder age was sorted out and integrated into the NHS, it hasn't happened. As a result, if you do lean on the state in your latter years you are likely to be bounced around between home, hospital and respite centres. At each stage the individual looking after you will be doing his/her best whilst their budget holder will be keeping them on a short rein and if it involves an NHS bed, there'll be someone in the background pressing for the bed to be released soonest for someone else. It works in a clumsy, clunky way and you will need to apply effort on your part, particularly to provide continuity between the helpful carers and nurses etc.

So if you can fund it yourself, that's going to be the way to go. You can then pick the circumstances of your care ie at home, in a care home or sheltered accommodation. You can determine who cares for you and whether that's only 30 minutes a day through to 24 hour live-in support. Sheltered accommodation is a popular option because it allows you to be on one site with others in a like time of life, whilst remaining independent. It will almost certainly offer 24/7 on site aid at the press of an emergency button, communal areas to meet and make friends and usually on-site dining. And if you want independence, your own front door. You'll also benefit from someone else taking care of maintenance as well as the feeling of safety. Against this, they usually don't want residents who already require regular medical assistance, often ban pets amongst some sometimes throttling rules, tend to come with high service charges and can be hard to resell. If this appeals, please do your research before taking the plunge. Is the location accessible for family and friends? Is it near shops etc? What do the existing residents think of the place? What realistically are the service charges, council tax and other outgoings likely to add up to?

State care is (at the time of writing) a responsibility of your local council. They are obliged to provide care if you need it, but not necessarily to pay for it. Determining who pays is by subjecting you to a 'means test'. If you have savings and other capital assets above a threshold of circa £23,250 you will be expected to pick up 100% of the costs. If your capital assets are less but your income will pay your bills and still allow you approx. £190 per week for yourself then again you will be asked to pay in full. Outside of these numbers there are sliding scales.

There are two other matters of concern to note with state paid care. Firstly, You cannot go for deliberate *deprivation of assets* - that is give away money specifically to make you poor enough for state aid. Secondly, your house is ignored for state aid purposes if you are receiving care at home or temporarily in a care home. If you move permanently into a care home, the authority will expect your house to be sold to pay for your care unless it is also the dwelling of your other half. If you are concerned about any of this, there is ample detail online.

PLAN B (a) Last will and testament

Talking about death is quite morbid. The problem is it is inevitable for all of us. Part of the reason why you bought this book was to make sure everything in your later life (and ultimately death) goes according to plan. But we all know that plans go awry, so we are now considering Plan B – a fall-back from the simple plan of carrying on living and enjoying life.

The first step is a will. Let's assume you haven't written one, although by now we really hope you have and it is up to date. A will can be handwritten or typed or printed, signed by you and witnessed by two independent people (eg neighbours) who don't benefit from it. Everything else is *nice to have* as opposed to legally necessary.

- You can buy a DIY will kit from most stationers, you can pay a lawyer to prepare one or go to a lawyer via a charity as many charities offer a free will-writing service if you're going to leave it money. You could simply write one yourself.
- It would be good to name an executor to act on the instructions in the will and perhaps an alternate should the first be unwilling or unable to act.
- If you leave everything to the other half – which is normal – also suggest what happens if they pre-decease you, eg split between the grandchildren.
- If your other half hasn't prepared a will, now would be a great time and it might be a good idea (but do

discuss) if theirs mirrored yours in terms of pre-decease and beneficiaries.

- Bear in mind if you both die together (horrible thought but accidents do happen)then under section 184 of the Law of Property Act 1925 the law deems that the elder of you to have died first. So if your wills differ beyond leaving everything to the other, then the younger of you two will have their will executed, having inherited from the older one.
- If you are leaving shares of your estate to children and grandchildren try and allow for additional ones arising between writing your will and your death and also for the contingency some of them die before you.
- Make sure the chosen executor and/or family etc know where you are keeping the original signed copy as that will be needed for probate and to act on your instructions.
- If you want to, you can also use the will to indicate how and where you wish to be buried, but that is probably something to discuss with the family separately in case funeral arrangements are necessary before anyone has read the will.
- Remarrying probably voids a will prepared beforehand other than in contemplation of the new marriage, so if you have a new partner, prepare a new will.
- You can prepare a new will at any time (with two witnesses) and for the sake of good order you should

mention the date of one it replaces and then ideally destroy the earlier one.

It's not nice considering your own mortality or the effect of the law on your will or the work of the executor or the possible squabbles between your next of kin – but if you are tidy now, things will be smoother after you are gone and for some, that's one less thing to worry about whilst you carry on with life.

Just as wills don't need to be prepared by a legal person, a legal professional is also only optional for probate. Probate, in case it is a strange concept to whoever is your executor, is proving the will is real and doing the accounting of your assets for the benefit primarily of Inheritance Tax. Probate is now largely an online form-filling exercise, and employing a solicitor to do it, still requires someone (usually the executor) to find all the answers eg house valuation, bank balance, value of shares etc, anyway – so why perhaps pay twice?

PLAN B (b) A living will

A living will is more properly known as a Lasting Power of Attorney (LPA) and authorises one or more individuals of your choosing (called the 'Attorneys') to manage on your behalf:

- Property and financial affairs – paying bills, selling property, managing investments and bank accounts etc; or
- Health and welfare – decisions on your care and in extremis when to call time on treatments etc; or
- both the above

if you are not capable yourself.

As with most of these things there is a fee for creating it and a government office – The Office of the Public Guardian - to register it and it can all be done online without legal help. And being government there are changing fee reductions and exemptions! And again, they request up to 10 weeks to do their end of things.

Another warning. To reiterate part of the purpose of this book is to act as a signpost. LPAs, like driving licences, state pensions and even travel visas can normally be obtained online directly from the government. So when you are being directed to the web, do take extra care to find the government site itself and not some internet entrepreneur's site which offers to help you with the process.

Only you know the answers to the questions that will be posed, so if you respond to an advert instead of the real site, you'll still need to find those answers anyway and it will cost you more – assuming they actually carry out the process at all.

Your Attorney(s) powers only exist if you are not capable – so under normal circumstances control of where you live, your assets and so on remain in your hands. And if for any reason you begin to doubt your choice of Attorney – rather than yourself – you can always cancel your LPA.

Obviously the right time to set up a LPA is when you are compos mentis and your signing hand produces a decent facsimile of your signature. Otherwise should you be incapacitated mentally or physically it might prove impossible to deal with impenetrable organisations like banks.

PLAN B (c) Provision for other(s)

If you are fortunate to have one (or more) occupational pensions offering final or average salary linked payouts, you are indeed one of a shrinking number of lucky individuals. At the time of writing with record low interest rates, pension annuity rates are also at an all-time low which means if you are having to buy yourself a pension then you will give up a lot of pounds for a smallish annual (or monthly) pension payment. The reverse is also true. It will be costing your ex-employer a lot of money to provide for your pension.

So your ex-employer would probably be overjoyed, if you are persuaded by someone looking to make a quick fee, if you wanted to withdraw the value of that pension and place it with another pension provider. That's because the cash in question is probably less than the full cost would otherwise likely to be for your ex-employer and is certainly so if someone takes out a fee on the way. So leaving it be, is often your best choice particularly as it is likely to increase its pay-out each year and there's probably a widow/widowers half pension paid if you die before your other half.

Several key points arise from that bland assertion:

- If you are single and proposing to stay that way, your pension pay-out is likely being held back by the provision of the half pension that'll never be paid. So maybe there is a negotiation?

- Conversely if you do have an other half, the half pension should be taken into account by you in making sure *their* income will suffice should you die first.
- At pension commencement you will doubtless be offered the choice to take up to a quarter of the pension in cash. Please consider this carefully again for several reasons:
  - Will you be comfortable on three quarters of the pension (plus other sources), particularly if the money is more useful now (maybe for the next generation) ?
  - Do you consider you can invest that sum and get a better return than the pension foregone - perhaps as tax-free ISAs - that might increase your total income?
  - Taking the money now means you have a lump sum should you ever need it, which isn't true with a pension ,if you pass up on the cash offer

PLAN B (d) Falling over – wake-up call

Have you ever woken up and said, to nobody in particular 'Oh, I certainly feel my age today'?

I think we all have at some time or another, but for the most part we go through life probably feeling younger than our calendar age. That being the case, there's got to be a time ahead of you when your body – probably more than your mind – has to do some catching up with reality.

UK annuity tables suggest that a man aged 65 today is likely to live on average to 85 with a 1 in 34 chance of reaching 100. A woman aged 65 is averagely living two more years and has a better, 1 in 20 chance of reaching three figures. So whilst I think we all want to be healthy until the day we die, the chances are (on average) in the 20 or 22 years from 65, we will deteriorate rather faster than in the first 65 years.

What this means is that we need to believe the old cliché: *it's better to do it today, than putting it off for tomorrow.* This applies to both some of the bigger issues raised in this book as much as what you might regard as housekeeping.

Now might be a very good time to give your finances a spring-clean:

- Do you have a list of your current investments and savings together with reference/customer/certificate numbers?

- Have you odd bank or building society accounts you have often meant to close but never made the effort?
- Have you gone carefully through your bank statement to see that you still really want and need each of the standing orders and direct debits that go out of your account every month, quarter or year?

And ask yourself, if you are not going to do it now or that the task seems impossible, when are you going to grasp the nettle and do it?

Likewise, there is no better time to deal with your home:

- Decoratively, and especially if it is going to be you with the paintbrush, why not bring the house up to scratch now as you might not touch it again in your lifetime?
- Do you want to install a personal alarm to alert others if you have an accident in the house and need to summon help? Sure, you don't need it now but must you fall over and not be able to get up first, before you make such an investment?
- How about the garden? Do you have thoughts of making it more easily maintained for the future? Paving or artificial grass instead of lawn perhaps? Raised flower beds and/or a greenhouse to potter in?
- Finally how about a clear out of everything you are just keeping because you haven't thrown it away. Or

kept *just in case*. Or it's those half used paint cans from how many years ago?

Tell you what – how about an incentive? Finally do what you have put off for so long, and then book yourself a holiday.

PLAN B (e) Level living

We've touched on the cash-flow advantages of downsizing and the health / care benefits of sheltered accommodation but there's more. If you live as most, in a house on two or more levels and you are determined to stay, you might now start considering some of the things that might assist you as you become older and less mobile. The Sunday papers are full of them: stair-lifts, walk-in baths, mobility scooters and so on. Not so widely advertised but of almost magical importance, if you don't already have one, is a downstairs toilet.

With a lump sum available from your pension you could probably have a lot of these things done now. But are you really fooling yourself? Are you trying to make a house designed for family living into a retirement home? It's time to think of level living.

Level living is for you to live and sleep on a single level. Not, unless you want to, one floor of your house where you then let the other to a lodger or to Airbnb visitor or whatever, but 'yes' a change of address to a bungalow or flat. It doesn't have to be downsizing in size or money but the advantages of everything on one level must be abundantly clear. Certainly when contemplating this, consider the advantages of location to be gained: near shops, close to family, beautiful scenery etc but also consider how a one level dwelling will not need expensive works to accommodate the later you.

Be careful that in choosing such a place that the level living extends to the world outside. Don't let the premises be a dozen steps up from the street, which might be no bother to you now but will increasingly be a problem when it comes to the bicycle you've promised to buy yourself or later on the mobility scooter. Having a flat beyond the ground floor should only be contemplated if there's a well maintained lift in place and provision for your bicycle etc at ground floor level.

Any relocation is a massive upheaval which most of us will have sworn to never do again after the last move. But ask yourself if for the next twenty years or so you are going to spend rather more time at home than the last 40 years, is this my ideal home? And if not swayed so far, think of the opportunity to de-clutter as you move out and reduced cleaning bills the other end. Think too of our off-quoted phrase *try before you buy.* Do rent a flat for a week somewhere close to where you are thinking of locating yourself and see if you like it before you firm up on your plans. Find the downsides beyond the simple things like not being able to find a tin-opener in the rented flat!

PLAN B (f) No time to die

'No time to die' was both a 1958 film (a second world war adventure) as well as the title of the James Bond movie whose launch was delayed by Covid19 – the Corona virus - of 2020. But there is a right time to die and that's when you have completed everything you want to achieve in life and to the extent you care, have your affairs for others to deal with post-death, in the best of order.

But it's not going to work out like that. Let's be both positive and defensive. On the positive front *now* would be a great time to generate a bucket list of things you'd like to achieve between now and whenever. Most bucket lists are full of travel desires: the Taj Mahal, Machu Picchu, Antarctica, Pisa, Bali, to name a few destinations. Perhaps to sail somewhere on a cruise liner or your own sail boat or something in between. To drive, motorbike or cycle Route 66 across the USA, or navigate the Panama Canal, or take the Trans-Siberian railway, or see Sloths in Madagascar, or Polar Bears in the Arctic. Simply drawing up the list is great fun, more so as you research a good time to go, how to do it with a reasonable budget, who to do it with and maybe even how to link two or more adventures together.

Bucket lists don't have to be exclusively travel or indeed refer to anything outside your house. The list could include learning something: a language, a dance, a musical instrument, a creative hobby, building a collection or growing a champion vegetable. You might want to write your memoirs, a novel or collate the stories you invented for your children. Maybe surprise yourself and learn to fly, ride a horse or gain a certificate in wine appreciation.

Then there are other people. Should your list include catching up with specific old friends who for whatever reason you've lost touch with? Places, hobbies, people, the limit is your imagination, tempered by what appeals and possibly what the budget will stand. And do make it open-ended. Feel free to add new aspirations and dreams and re-order the priority of them any time.

Defensively, having spring-cleaned your finances a couple of chapters ago, how about bringing all your paperwork in one place? Most of us don't have fireproof safes so how about acquiring a simple metal filing box? I say 'metal' because you probably would like it to survive should, heaven forbid, the house burns down, or is hit by a piece of space junk etc. Into the box put the following:

- Your will (or a copy if the original is held somewhere else)
- A list of your computer and phone passwords and codes
- Copies of bank statements (and if you are 'paperless' a print out of the details)
- Copies of insurance policies
- Share certificates, title deeds and other documents of ownership
- Spare keys

- Photocopies of your bank and credit cards
- Copy of your picture page of passport and of your driving licence

And what is really useful, but rarely done, would be one page in calendar date order of everything in the box that has a renewal date (including passport and driving licence) so that if for some reason a renewal doesn't show up, you'll know when to chase.

HAPPY RETIREMENT

Michael Carter – Author

Michael qualified as a Chartered Accountant with KPMG in London in 1978. His career then saw him typically became Finance Director for a succession of companies in the UK, often with US parents, across industries like vending, software and telecoms.

Michael was part of the team that delivered the first Internet on TV. He invented a vending system that sold seven million cups within a year. His entrepreneurship has also run to solving business problems, like finding buyers for companies when the only alternative was closure.

With a taste for independence, Michael began as a business consultant and has now worked with over fifty clients, providing help with planning, fundraising, share option schemes, quiet advice for CEOs and several roles as part-time Finance Director.

Many would-be start-ups have enlisted help and advice from Michael. Ever up for a new challenge, he began writing business books in 2004 to address some of the common issues he found with his clients.

This led to other books – a novel trilogy, a nonsense story and some collaborations. This is his eleventh book.

Thanks for buying it.

Printed in Great Britain
by Amazon

27854793R00036